CUSTOMER LOYALTY

Forthcoming titles in this series will include

- *Winning Sales Letters*
- *Win–Win Negotiation*
- *How to Wow and Audience*
- *Make the Most of Meetings*
- *Key Account Management*
- *Coping with Company Politics*
- *Winning CVs*
- *How to Pay Less Tax*

Do you have ideas for subjects which could be included in this exciting and innovative series? Could your company benefit from close involvement with a forthcoming title?

Please contact David Grant Publishing Limited
80 Ridgeway, Pembury, Tunbridge Wells, Kent TN2 4EZ
Tel/Fax +44 (0)1892 822886
Email GRANTPUB@aol.com
with your ideas or suggestions.

BUILDING
CUSTOMER LOYALTY

John Frazer-Robinson

60 Minutes Success Skills Series

Copyright © John Frazer-Robinson 1999

First published 1999 by
David Grant Publishing Limited
80 Ridgeway
Pembury
Kent TN2 4EZ
United Kingdom
Tel/Fax +44 (0)1892 822886
Email GRANTPUB@aol.com

01 00 99   10 9 8 7 6 5 4 3 2 1

60 Minutes Success Skills Series is an imprint of
David Grant Publishing Limited

All rights reserved. Except for the quotation of short passages for the purposes of criticism and review, no part of this publication may be reproduced, stored in a retrieval system, or transmitted, in any form or by any means, electronic, mechanical, photocopying, recording or otherwise, without the prior permission of the publisher.

British Library Cataloguing in Publication Data
A CIP catalogue record for this book is available from the British Library

ISBN 1-901306-27-5

Cover design: Liz Rowe
Text design: Graham Rich
Production coordinator: Paul Stringer
Edited and Typeset in Futura by Kate Williams
Printed and bound in Great Britain by
T.J. International Ltd, Padstow, Cornwall

This book is printed on acid-free paper

The publishers accept no responsibility for any investment or financial decisions made on the basis of the information in this book. Readers are advised always to consult a qualified financial adviser.

All names mentioned in the text have been changed to protect the identity of the business people involved. Any resemblance to existing companies or people is entirely coincidental.

Contents

Welcome: About *Building Customer Loyalty*   7

Chapter 1: What's important about Customer loyalty?   9
The facts and fallacies of Customer loyalty
The ultimate measure of your success
The five strands of true loyalty

Chapter 2: Think bigger, Think better, Think Customer!   21
What wins hearts and minds?
Customer thinking is a way of life
The Age of the Customer

Chapter 3: The nine steps to profitable loyalty building   29
Managing Customer loyalty
Understanding defectors
All Customers are not equal
The role of complaints and complaint handling

Chapter 4: How do you measure loyalty?   39
Measuring loyalty
Involving your Customers
The four dimensions of loyalty
Getting your team on board

Chapter 5: The Customer-driven business model   47
Be Customer-driven
17 key issues for Customer loyalty
Formal and informal referrals

Chapter 6: Kick-starting the Loyalty Process   55
Where to start
Re-tuning your mind . . . and your money
The Time Tested Time Test

WELCOME!

ABOUT *BUILDING CUSTOMER LOYALTY*

Greetings! Welcome to this book about the hottest topic in sales and marketing – Customer loyalty. However powerful Customer loyalty is, you will fail to maximise the full value for your business unless you have a strategy, manage Customer loyalty properly and inculcate a Customer-centred culture into your whole business.

> *" I firmly believe that people buy people.*
> *And loyal staff breed loyal Customers. "*
> **– Moyra Wood, Business Manager, L&M Ltd**

Customer loyalty cannot be built just by sales and marketing people – although they can do a lot towards it and later chapters will explain much more on the marketing role in loyalty building. The Customer's experience embraces the whole business and therefore the whole business has to think and breath loyalty. Thus, for example, you will find that your staff or colleagues are major contributors to effective loyalty building.

How does this book work?

To begin with, settle yourself somewhere quiet and comfortable and read the entire book. Next, use the book for reference. When you need some help, glance through it to remind yourself of all the various ideas and thoughts. Lastly, refresh your ideas by using the book on an ongoing basis. Why not re-read a different chapter each month until you feel you have absorbed it totally?

If you are an old friend of this series, you will find a new kind of feature panel in this book: the STORY panel. The point of these real-life stories is to make you aware of all the exciting Customer things that are going on out there. That's the way your competition is thinking and behaving. To create loyal Customers – people who won't even think about going anywhere else – you are going to have to beat your competition hands down. To choose not to is quite simply to sign your own corporate death warrant.

About the 60 Minutes series

The 60 Minutes Success Skills Series is written for people with neither the time nor the patience to trawl through acres of jargon, management-speak and page-filling waffle. Like all the books in the series, *Building Customer Loyalty* has been written in the belief that you can learn all you really need to know quickly and without hassle. The aim is to distil the essential, practical advice you can use straight away.

Good luck!

What's important about Customer loyalty?

Coming up in this chapter

The facts and fallacies of Customer loyalty
The ultimate measure of your success
The five strands of true loyalty

> " When Customers buy your products or services their experience is not just with the sales team but with the whole business and therefore the whole business has to think and breath loyalty. "
> – **George Sanders, MD, high street stationery retailer**

The facts and fallacies of Customer loyalty

Many marketing experts of our time seem to be taking simple long-held marketing knowledge and beliefs and making them more complex than they actually are. Some manage to find ways of explaining and describing fundamental truths in the most complex fashions. In relation to Customer satisfaction and Customer loyalty there seems to be a lot of this going on. I remain undecided. Is it really getting more complex as we move further into the "soft" emotional issues of Customer relationships and the genuine intricacies of the human psychological aspects come into closer focus? Or are my peers and I guilty of complicating very simple issues? Maybe some of both is true – I will leave you to decide for yourself as you digest this chapter.

> " *Loyalty is about what Customers do, not what they say. This is an important distinction for your business. You must realise that it makes Customer satisfaction (what I might say: "Yes, it's fine, thank you") deeply subordinate to Customer loyalty (what I actually do: "I'm not coming here again").* "
> – **James Tremain, Customer Services Director**

BUILDING CUSTOMER LOYALTY

> **The waitress was a singer**
>
> I was on the road home. It was late and I was hungry. I soon sat in the rather shabby branch of a chain of British roadside restaurants. I chewed my way through a very tasteless and rather tough piece of steak which was marginally better than staying hungry. About half way through the young waitress who had taken my order and served me, reappeared. She sang to me, "Is everything alllIriiight?"
>
> I don't know who teaches people to sing to their Customers. Switchboard operators and receptionists do it too. It's as if they equate the singing tone and extended vowels with a caring attitude. I looked at her, smiled and replied, "Yes, it's fine thank you". She had just sampled Customer satisfaction. It showed 100 per cent satisfaction.
>
> The truth was that the steak was well below acceptable and I was actually toying with the idea of re-soling a pair of favourite old shoes with the remains of it. My real reply should have been, "No – it's awful and I'm not coming here again". Customer loyalty index? Zero.
>
> Well, why didn't I tell her? Because, because. Because I was tired. She was at the end of her shift. They were waiting to close. I couldn't be bothered. It wasn't her fault. And so on. You know how it is! But I still won't go back there.

Plenty of people will tell you that satisfaction levels are linked to loyalty levels. That's rather like saying that a swimming pool *looks* warm enough. There is nothing better than actually sticking a toe in and feeling it to find out. Of course they are linked. There would be little loyalty without Customer satisfaction.

However, managing Customer satisfaction is not enough. It is, as you will read, just one of the components. You have to get Customers well towards the very top end of satisfaction levels before there is any kind of robustness where loyalty is created.

> You are looking for a restaurant to take someone special. Turning to a colleague at work you say "How was that new French place in Hopnall Street; the one you went to last week?"
> "Yeah, I was satisfied."
> Satisfied? Is that the best it gets? Customer satisfaction is

just not enough. The scale of the word doesn't reach high enough. I prefer the description "actively satisfied", meaning so deliriously happy they go around telling people how great their experience was. We'll come back to this.

The inescapable truth of Customer loyalty

Loyalty is essential for the success of your whole business, and nothing but success can be used to measure and judge the effectiveness of Customer loyalty. It is the sum total of the effect of your business or organisation on its Customers and their response to it. This means that the Customer is, and must always be, the reason for your existence; you can have no other reason. In business we have no other purpose; it is the inexorable rationale for the Customer-driven business. It explains why it is quite wrong to stand up in front of staff and tell them that they are the most important asset of the business. They clearly are not. The Customer has to be first and foremost because without Customers, who needs staff? Any business leader with enough money can certainly have as many staff as they like with no Customers at all – but not many of them make that choice!

Employees come number two in a Customer-driven business. And not just front line employees, but all employees. This means that the culture in which they all work has to be a Customer first culture, even in the depths of the back office. For a business to succeed with Customer loyalty, you can have no defaulters – anywhere.

A while ago I was running a group of businesses and I wrote this maxim, which we used as our creed:

The object of a business is not to make money.
The object of a business is to serve its Customers.
The result is to make money.

I use this maxim with all the businesses I work with. This spirit becomes embedded into their culture. Why? Because all my experience has been that those who sit around counting pennies when they could be concentrating

BUILDING CUSTOMER LOYALTY

everything on getting it right for Customers make so much less money than the ones who make Customers their passion, their obsession. People flock to these businesses.

Don't make the mistake of trying to make as much money as possible; it is the most limiting mistake you can make. Just concentrate on Customers. Now, ask yourself, what difference will this make to the way you do business?

Satisfaction may be a vital component part of Customer loyalty, yet as well as dissatisfied Customers, satisfied Customers leave your business and defect. More confusing still, loyal Customers leave you too. In fact, my wife Elaine and I have just parted company with a host of traders, shops and services to whom we were totally loyal and about whom we would still give excellent word of mouth referrals. We just moved house and changed area.

Did you hear about the Canadian bank who sent out a survey to Customers who had closed their account? "How satisfied were you?" they asked. Then they sat back and waited for the proverbial to hit the fan. I mean these people obviously weren't happy, they had closed their account!

80% of them claimed to be totally satisfied! True story.

So they went back again and asked, "Well, if you were so satisfied, why did you close the account?" Almost 80% of the 80% said that something had gone wrong with, or during, a transaction in the bank branch – a people failure or a service failure. So they shut the account and stomped out. There's just no getting away from getting your act right.

The five strands that create Customer Loyalty

The five strands of Customer loyalty are:

- price
- product
- delivery
- service
- recognition

WHAT'S IMPORTANT ABOUT CUSTOMER LOYALTY?

Each strand needs careful thought. I have a PowerPoint slide which lists these five. In order to make a point, I listed the five with the first two – price and product – in white and the last two – service and recognition – in red. Delivery is in half white and half red. "Why", I ask my audiences, "do you think delivery is half white and half red?"

What's the answer? Not what someone proposed recently. "You're no good at PowerPoint!", he ventured. No, Sir!

So what is the answer? It's that the issues wrapped round the first two and a half strands – price, product and some delivery issues – are based in logic. The other two and a half – the remainder of delivery, service and recognition – are based in emotion. For the past 30 years, marketing has obsessed itself with the first two and a half. Now, in order to concentrate on Customer relationships you have to get your business to become excellent at delivering the emotionally based issues.

> **You are what you eat**
>
> You may have heard that expression used about food. Eat fat – get fat, so they say. Well, the same applies to your business. So, if you sell on price, you attract people who buy on price. If they buy on price, next time they'll buy the cheapest elsewhere. If you want to be the bargain basement of your particular market, go for it! If not, beware! Customers who come for price, go for price. They have little long-term loyalty potential.

Customer loyalty and Customer satisfaction both share the same five strands. The five things entwine like the strands of a rope. They are:

1. Price

There's no getting away from price. It is always there in, what I call, "the value balance". However, very often we overrate the importance of price – or, worse still, we actually exacerbate it. If you are generally a discount or bargain basement operation, that's fine. If not, you are simply eroding your own margins by promoting on price. This does not stop you promoting on value.

thirteen

BUILDING CUSTOMER LOYALTY

But get price in perspective. One of the long-term reasons for adopting a Customer loyalty strategy is that it shrinks price in the Customer's priority and replaces it with value.

> I once met a man who owned a small chain of supermarkets. He had his Customer loyalty programme – a computer-based combination of Customer care, communications and, significantly, purchase tracking – to such a fine art he could even prompt and remind Customers who had forgotten regular purchases. He even had a delivery service for them when they were sick. How did he know they were sick? He rang them when his database showed they hadn't been to the store on one of their usual days! He had endless stories of the things his business did for Customers.
>
> I asked him "How do you deliver all that service and still keep your price in line with your competitors? They are always cutting margins." Smiling broadly he replied, "They have to. But my Customers don't come to me for the lowest prices. They don't come to me for what they can buy. They come because of what we do for them and how special we make them feel! We haven't cut a margin in years!"

2. Product

There is no substitute for delivering a quality product. If the product fails, breaks down, doesn't last as long as it should or is in any way imperfect, Customers will not come back for more. Nor will they feel inclined to buy other things from you. One of the stark realisations a Customer-driven business has to make from the very beginning is that there are no hiding places. Customer loyalty is built by *exceeding* Customer expectations at every opportunity.

> Following spinal surgery, I acquired a new work station and chair which enable me to continue to work long hours at my PC. The screen and keyboard are raised, encouraging me to sit correctly for my spine. It was a self-build or "flatpack", which I quickly constructed with the simple instructions – the only kind that are any good for me! To the right of the

WHAT'S IMPORTANT ABOUT CUSTOMER LOYALTY?

> keyboard support was a mouse shelf which I could not get to stay in position. One day, since the manufacturer was local, I decided to take the faulty parts to them. I was greeted with profuse apologies, offered coffee and asked to wait a few minutes. The factory manager arrived carrying the unit, now with mouse tray correctly attached saying, "I want you to know how grateful we are to you for taking the time to visit us and bring us this defective product. I can assure you defects are rare but you have enabled us to uncover a batch of keyboard supports which have brackets three millimetres out of alignment. Thanks to you we can contact the relevant dealers and recall the units and rescue our reputation for perfection. I have a meeting in ten minutes time with my production team to see how we can stop such an error happening again." More pleasantries followed and I went on my way a happy Customer. And I'd buy from them again – or recommend them to anyone.

3. Delivery

If you are an "old school" marketer or sales person and are familiar with the old textbooks, this is what used to be called "distribution". If you have some of the old textbooks, throw them away or hide them in the loft. Marketing has changed so much over the past few years that the old ideas no longer work. Or do they? We'll come back to this.

> For some time now, I have been telling one or two stories about Marriott Hotels' Customer initiative. "Just ask", they say. So if you arrive at Seattle Airport and suddenly realise you left your briefcase in the restaurant, phone the restaurant manager, explain your problem and he'll fix it. You get your briefcase back.
>
> Often the Marriott person who owns the problem will actually accompany the item and, as they hand it over will ask where you are going. As you reveal your destination they ask, "Can I book you into the Marriott?" Many Customers feel churlish saying no and, of course, Marriott is happy to fix the cancellation of any prior booking.
>
> One of my workshop attendees, Bruce McNeely, had been a Marriott Customer on his way to the workshop – he was

> returning from Canada to Dubai. He went for a quick session in the Calgary Marriott hotel gym before he checked out, leaving his wedding and signet rings in his room for safety. You've guessed! He told me how they sent a chambermaid to search for them, she located the rings and a taxi went from the hotel to the airport where they were handed over. "It must have set them back about thirty two bucks in cab fares," smiled Bruce, "and they wouldn't accept a cent".

Delivery includes distribution but it encompasses far more. Think of it as the delivery of the whole corporate promise to the Customer. By this I mean every facet of the way the Customer feels, touches and experiences your business. This includes the way the call centre or switchboard deal with Customers, the wording on your packaging, owners' manuals or handbooks, the impact of your invoices and stationery, the way you announce price increases, your attitude to "green" issues and genetic modification of food, if appropriate. Everything makes an impression on a Customer, so make sure it's a great impression.

> *I loved the software but the manual was hopeless. I wouldn't buy anything of their's again.*
> – **George Elphick, accountancy specialist**

The significant difference between distribution and delivery is the realisation that when you market to achieve a series of separate transactions those transactions take place at the far point of your distribution channel. This is a product-driven process. It distributes your corporate product or service. When you market to achieve a managed Customer relationship, then what we have is a means of delivering the corporate promise. Transaction marketing effectively switches on to standby between transactions; relationship marketing is permanently fully switched on for twenty-four hours a day, seven days a week, ready and alert to every Customer interaction, wherever it touches the organisation.

4. Service

In a Customer-driven business, service is paramount – but by now you should be getting the impression that everything is

WHAT'S IMPORTANT ABOUT CUSTOMER LOYALTY?

paramount, which is why I said earlier that a Customer loyalty strategy must obsess the whole business. If you are a small business, this is good news. Both size and structure inhibit larger businesses delivering service. Smaller companies don't have nearly so many protocols and are much less set in their ways. If a Customer wants something different or special, they can just do it.

Does this mean a big business cannot become a Customer-driven business? Certainly not! But it does mean it has more, and more serious, issues to address — management culture, organisational structure, human resources, to name but a few. In short, they have to retain the advantages of size and lose the disadvantages. Lumbering giants have to become as agile and fleet of foot as their smaller competitors.

> At the same workshop as Bruce McNeely was Masoud Mohammed Saleh, head of the Dubai Department of Civil Aviation marketing team. Masoud told me he had a great Customer service story. See what you think.
>
> Masoud, complete with his wife and their infant child, were in the middle of an almost round the world trip with Lufthansa. Arriving at Frankfurt he secured his own bag and his wife's from the belt. But the brightly coloured rucksack belonging to the little one was not there. A baggage handler, spotting their plight, hurried off to find the supervisor from Lufthansa. She arrived. "What was in the bag, Sir?"
>
> "Actually, not much," replied Masoud, "but it was important. The baby's milk for the trip and Pampers." The Lufthansa rep asked more questions including, curiously, the baby's doctor's phone number in Dubai. Masoud, puzzled, obliged with the number.
>
> Ten minutes passed. Back came the Lufthansa lady with their Frankfurt Manager of Customer Service. "Sorry we took so long," they explained, "but we wanted to call your doctor because the type of milk your baby drinks, we don't have here. This brand he has approved. And here is a box of Pampers. Make the baby comfortable, then we'll go and buy a nice new bag."
>
> For the rest of the trip, at every destination, Masoud and his family were treated to free Pampers and a free supply of milk approved by their family doctor. The airline said "We fixed the problem, but we haven't said sorry to our little

> Customer yet. We have decided your baby will enjoy a 75% ticket discount on Lufthansa for life."
>
> This is a great win–win situation, with very impressed Customers for whom Lufthansa will be the family first choice for decades, and maybe even generations.

5. Recognition

Whether you're thinking about Customer loyalty for business to business or business to consumer, the rudiments of developing and managing Customer loyalty are exactly the same. We all love to be recognised not just for who we are but for other things about us.

One of the biggest contributions I have seen to the loyalty building process has come from streaming consistent groups of employees to consistent groups of Customers. The result is that the two groups become familiar with each other and their relationships have a far greater chance of success. They know each other!

> Shortly after my wife, Elaine, and I got together we decided to travel back to my old stomping ground where my mother and brother still live. It was time to let them in on the fact we had decided to marry. I asked them both to join us for lunch, together with my son and his partner. To book a table, I rang a restaurant that used to be a haunt, but where I hadn't been for the best part of 12 or more years. Paul, the owner of the Bella Vista, answered the phone and, as soon as I announced myself, the years dissolved as if they had never been. We had some catching up time and then I told Paul that I would like a table for six the following Sunday. "Sure," he said, "would you like your usual table?" Not bad after 12 years!

To boost Customer loyalty, we therefore need to work on continuous improvement of the corporate promise and that means all five strands of it. It means adding to our previous experiences, which were logic based – product, price and some delivery issues (essentially those to do with distribution) – and supplementing them with new, "soft issue" experiences, which are emotionally based – service, recognition and the corporate delivery issues that surround the product at distribution and stay connected with the Customer throughout their relationship with you. Now we have to examine how we leave Customers feeling.

For those who worry that this is new and different, it is not. It has been done before – but not in the volume and at the speed required today. For my parents, for example, the kind of things we are discussing in this book were not only the ideals to which they worked, they were what they expected – and got – even if it was low tech or no tech!

1. Loyalty has to be the desire, mission, passion and obsession of the whole business. Only a business wholly committed to loyalty will succeed.
2. Customer satisfaction is what people say: loyalty is what they do. Customer loyalty is the ultimate measure of how well your business is delivering its whole corporate promise.
3. The five strands of loyalty are price, product, delivery, service and recognition. Price and product are logical issues whereas service and recognition are emotional. Delivery is both.
4. Marketing is moving into the soft issues – the emotional content of the Customer relationship. How do we leave Customers feeling?

THINK BIGGER, THINK BETTER, THINK CUSTOMER!

Chapter 2

Coming up in this chapter

Will bribery work?
What wins hearts and minds?
Customer thinking is a way of life
The Age of the Customer

To increase Customer loyalty all you have to do is think bigger and better. And that means it is important to shift from thinking about Customers as units of transaction – single sales – and start treating them as individuals you want to have a Customer relationship with for life. "Life" in this context may not mean for the whole of the Customer's life – but in some cases, it might.

> " *We market a chain of disco's and night clubs for the late teens, early twenties. By twenty five our Customer's life is over!* "
> – **Nicki Gage, marketing executive, Inn Places**

One of the world's largest motor manufacturers worked out the true value of a new Customer and realised it was not just the purchase of their next car but actually over £400,000. Huh?

They figured that if you add in all the potential repeat purchases, all the servicing, all the finance, all the extras – if they got their act right all the way through – that was the potential value to the brand. Seeing a person entering your door as a potential Customer with a lifetime value of £400,000 rather than just a £15,000 transaction can lead to some valuable shifts in thinking.

> What changes when you think about the value of that Customer to your business for the long term and have them spend all their potential money with you? How will thinking like this change your view, your attitude, tactics, marketing, thinking, service – everything?

BUILDING CUSTOMER LOYALTY

Bribery and integrity are like oil and water – they don't mix!

Most loyalty programmes rely, to a major degree, on bribery. This is like the villain in a children's pantomime handing out sweets to the goody in the show. None of the kids in the audience are fooled. They don't trust the villain's smile or voice.

> " We've had Customers coming here for 30 years and their parents often came before them. Families don't come back to businesses for 50 years out of habit. They come back because we constantly, constantly impress them. We knock their socks off! "
> – **Monty Goldsmith, managing director, Crouch Tailoring**

Loyalty building is about gathering the emotional commitment of the Customer so that they bestow their allegiance to you. It is about winning over the hearts and minds of Customers. Most of the so-called loyalty programmes are disguised sales promotions which use the mail and the shop and whatever to merchandise special offers and discounts. It's basically good, old-fashioned bribery – targeted sales promotion. This may *satisfy* Customers, but it won't build robust loyalty.

I often ask audiences the following. First I ask those who have a loyalty card to raise their hands. Then I ask those who do not have two or more loyalty cards for the same type of business – supermarket, hotel group, airline – to lower their hands. Lastly, I ask of the remaining raised hands, who uses all the businesses and frequently gathers loyalty bonuses from all the programmes? There are still many hands showing.

To which company are these people being loyal?

My next question is, "If you found your partner had two or more other people to whom he or she was also being 'loyal' on a regular basis, would you consider he or she was also being 'faithful'? If you do, keep your hands up." I haven't had one yet.

The truth is that, at best, these schemes only create a bond; just a link, not a lock. Some may manage a reasonably strong bond. The major benefit of such schemes is that they tend to increase exposure to, and sampling of, the corporate promise. I use my airline miles or storecard bonus points for more of what I have been getting already. I'll fly somewhere on holiday or buy something, which means the operator of the loyalty scheme gets another chance to prove their worth.

So, what wins hearts and minds?

Certainly, there is a place for discounts and special deals if they fit with your mission and your brand(s). However, the bulk of the loyalty building solutions will be found in the soft issues to do with service and recognition. It may be considered occasionally right or prudent to issue money off vouchers or make discount offers, but it is also to do with the style and tone of voice or offer with which they are distributed on those occasions.

In delivering those aspects of the corporate promise to do with service and recognition, the hearts and minds will be won over. Recognise and treat Customers as the individuals they are, know their preferences and choices, understand what turns them on or off. This builds loyalty – and it also creates a "quality lock", which locks them to you and locks your competitors out. Further, knowing Customers' preferences – indeed accumulating and actively using information in recognition of that Customer – means the Customer has taken you through a learning cycle about themselves. They have, effectively, trained you to look after them. That should make you easier and more convenient to deal with and others less so. It is a sort of golden ring-fence. It keeps the Customer with you and the others out; part of the quality lock.

> I was asked to carry out a marketing audit for a financial services business in the UK. They felt they had incredibly "loyal" Customers. They had over 150,000 policyholders of whom only 7,000 had bought more than one product. Now they may have had a good image with Customers. They may have great Customer satisfaction. But loyalty? They were kidding themselves.

Switching to a loyalty mind-set means turning much more attention on your Customers. They won't become more loyal unless you devote more time and effort to them. But the result is not just a good warm feeling, the result is increased sales at far lower costs. That's why you have to get into the loyalty business.

And to get into the loyalty business, we have to do loyalty work. Loyalty work is real. It happens in Customers lives. It's attentive to Customers and it builds far more for you than any disguised bribery via a simple loyalty club, programme, or scheme. Why? Because Customers feel it, experience it, and value it. It's a much more tangible demonstration of the way you value them and their custom than a few mailings and a sporadic dissemination of discount vouchers from manufacturers you have been able to do deals with. Customers have been there and done that. It's called the past. Customers realise that now what is happening is about them, driven by and for their needs, aspirations and desires – and it is happening in tune with their lives.

> Think about the implication of this for your business.
>
> A European insurance company were coming to the end of their year. They called me in because their sales were less than half their targets. After a look at things I sat with the CEO, marketing director and sales director. "The answer is simple," I suggested. "There is no loyalty work going on at all. As of tomorrow we start to concentrate on building Customer loyalty. As of now, I propose we ban, on pain of dismissal, any sales person from going near anyone who isn't already a Customer." With a loyalty focus sales went through the roof. The following year they sold over double their expectation. Just as important, Customer retention also improved radically. It was quick too. The "turn" came in less than three months!

Loyalty is so much more robust than satisfaction. It permits dialogue. It tolerates flaws as long as they are sensitively handled, tangible action is taken to avoid them happening again and the apologies are sincere.

This makes the Customer relationship paramount. But that is good news and far less daunting than people perceive. Because Customer relationships hold no mystery.

> With some of my conference audiences I ask them to examine the difference between a personal relationship and a commercial relationship. I use role play, selecting a person from the audience. I say someone; I've never picked on a man yet! We flirt, get to know each other, fall in love and decide to get married. We also have a row and break up. Whether we have a divorce or get back together is left for the woman to decide. This is an entertaining way to look at the phases of the relationship and to highlight the similarities. We find that the content of Customer relationships and personal relationships may be different, but the process is not. The phases of the relationship are identical.

Make Customer thinking a way of life in your business

I have produced a business model which takes you through the whole Customer-driven process. From the model it becomes clear how all the steps fit together in a virtuous, complementary fashion to improve the lot of the Customer and build Customer loyalty. The results also simultaneously lower marketing and sales costs, improve brand performance and increase business efficiency as a part of an holistic continuum. It also demonstrates that many aspects must come together to work in harmony so that the Customer wins all the way through – and, just as importantly, so do you! The model has a chapter all to itself towards the end of the book. It is explained in detail there.

So why is all this happening?

Two forces are coming together to change the way we do things. Firstly, Customers have realised that they have the money, therefore they have the choice of where and how to spend it. They are in control. For example, if you consider that my parents had to wait six months for a black and white television to watch the coronation of Queen Elizabeth II and compare that with the situation now, you will understand why I explain that many markets have come through the "Age of Plenty" to reach the "Age of Sufficiency". This also means, if we are in any "age" at all, then really it is the "Age of the Customer".

BUILDING CUSTOMER LOYALTY

The second force is the opportunity and ability created by the combination of computers, telephony and digital communications. Bring these two powerful forces together and you are on the perfect starting block for a Customer-focused culture, attitude and environment.

> A few years ago, I took a suite in a hotel on Park Lane. I was attending the British Direct Marketing Awards. It was a *great* night; a once in a lifetime. I collected six or seven certificates, five trophies and the coveted gold award. A real event for me since it made me the only person to have received the "gold" twice in the entire history of the awards.
>
> At around 4am I tottered into my hotel. I was showered with greetings and congratulations. There and then it seemed that everyone on night duty was joining in. When I checked out next day, I made a point of thanking the manager for his kind hand-written note which had been delivered on my breakfast tray.
>
> A year passed; a year when I only used the hotel once after my "gold" night. How do you think I felt when the front desk clerk greeted me like this?
>
> "Mr Frazer-Robinson. We are so pleased to have you back with us again. We checked with your secretary, and she said it was awards night. So we've given you the same suite as last year. It seemed so lucky for you."
>
> How did I feel? GREAT! So what is this? Salesmanship? Professionalism? Excellence? Yes, it is undoubtedly all those things. It's also note-taking, record-keeping, and a great deal of belief in the very highest standards of relationships.

As one of the US supermarket chains says:

Rule 1: the Customer is always right.
Rule 2: when the Customer is wrong, go back to Rule 1.

1. Think bigger – think better – think Customer! Why go for one sale when you can gain a Customer for life?
2. Loyalty is not about bribery. It is about how successfully you build valuable, lasting relationships with your Customers – winning their hearts and minds.

3. The processes of personal and Customer relationships are similar, even though the content is different.
4. Marketing is returning to the Customer values of old. It must do so because two forces are driving change. Firstly, the Customer has realised they are King. Secondly, marketers have the benefits of modern computing, telephony and digital communications.

THE NINE STEPS TO PROFITABLE LOYALTY BUILDING

Chapter 3

Coming up in this chapter

Managing Customer loyalty
Understanding defectors
All Customers are not equal
The role of complaints and complaint handling

Managing Customer loyalty

Let's look together at the nine steps you should take to build and manage loyalty for your business.

1. Define, then manage loyalty

Every business has its own idea of what is meant by loyalty and, probably, different shades of it. So create your own definition but be very sure that your definition includes measurable performance indicators. You'll find some ideas for measurement in the following chapter, so you can decide which, if not all, of those are appropriate for your business and/or add your own.

> If you can't measure loyalty, then you can't manage it. You're driving blind!

Remember to set your sights high. Our task is to exceed Customers' expectations at every interaction because this will lead to active satisfaction, which is very powerful and builds loyalty.

2. Understand the economics of loyalty

Here's what happens. Price sensitivity goes down. Referrals go up. Sales costs go down. It sounds good! But we need to know by how much. Start with a clear audit of what's happening now — otherwise you won't know just how clever you have been! If it's possible audit the business Customer by Customer. If not, use the smallest possible homogeneous groups. To provide an effective audit you should take soundings on the same performance indicators that you built in to your definition in Step 1.

3. Segment and identify high loyalty potential Customers

Are you choosing the right Customers? This concept surprises people and I still don't know why. You have to be choosy about who you let be a Customer of yours. Most businesses go at markets as if they were vacuum cleaners. They'll suck up anything. The fact is most businesses have Customers who range in value — some are extremely profitable, some are loss-making and there are some on whom you may be lucky to break even. If you can't manage those in the last two groups successfully into profit, politely and sensitively move them on.

4. Re-focus marketing investment and acquisition activity accordingly

Now you have cleaned out your Customer base examine the exquisite remainder closely. They are your most valuable group of Customers — the ones who are your most profitable. What do you see? Look for facts about them that they have in common; things like age, gender, location, income, wealth, job type. Or if it's a business, size, sector, and so on. Make up a profile of these Customers and you now have a profile of the kind of Customers who have the highest loyalty potential for you. Aren't these the Customers you want most? Now re-focus all your efforts on attracting more "perfect" Customers to your business. What about the others? Let your competitors lose money on them!

5. Align personnel recruitment, motivation and rewards to Customer values

Now you have to make sure your business is manned to suit these perfect Customers. I remember when, before regulation, insurance businesses would recruit almost anyone to sell for them. Most of them would be the very last person you would place your savings or pension with.

THE NINE STEPS TO PROFITABLE LOYALTY BUILDING

> A German chain store, Netto, recently explained how it's basic market was mature adults and a survey of Customers had revealed they most like to be served by (surprise, surprise!) mature adults.

Next, look at how you motivate your people. If you want to read more about motivation, you'll find some information in other books in this series: *High Performance Sales Management* and another devoted entirely to motivation, *Mastering Motivation*.

> Be particularly aware of commission on sales. It is perfectly good to build up the commission kitty from sales, but don't pay it out that way. Dispense it against things that work for Customers – Customer satisfaction, loyalty levels, decreases in Customer loss rates, increasing share of spend, increasing product or service sales across the range, complaint-free periods, and so on.
>
> Also think about who you include with the rewards. A lot more people contribute to building Customer loyalty than just the sales person.

6. Develop management thinking, processes and systems which actively improve retention rates

Make sure that the whole business – and yes, I do mean whole business – is geared to Customer retention and development. That means accounts, personnel, everywhere. Make sure, also, that all managers realise that the most important activity happens at the front line but everyone's contribution is vital.

> Managers of front line people are there to enable not to meddle. Managers have to get rid of problems for Customer-facing staff; to move barriers. When a barrier is too big for them to handle on their own, a director should roll his sleeves up and help shift it. This is a seriously Customer-driven culture and creates a great motivational atmosphere to work in.

7. Probe and understand defectors' behaviour and reasoning

Above all, go and talk to defectors! This is what I call those who decide they don't want to be your Customer any more. There are acceptable reasons for defection – moving out of the area is one – and unacceptable reasons – a failure of some kind, even if it is only in the Customers' perception. Failures must be removed or eradicated – and apologised for. Your long-term goal is a zero rate of the unacceptable kind of defection. Ideally, no Customer loss should occur without:

- you knowing about it
- the Customer being able and encouraged to tell you why they have made that choice
- learning from the experience so that any problem can be fixed.

Lastly, the Customer should be appropriately thanked for both their help and their custom.

8. Set loyalty targets and analyse your results

Go back to the performance indicators that were developed as part of your definition of loyalty in Step 1. Set achievable but stretching targets for these based on the audit carried out in Step 2. Use these to analyse just how well you are doing and what the trends are. The nearer you can get to doing this *per Customer,* the better. The review process should be regular and continuous. If you are not achieving targets, find out why not. What action needs to be taken? Will training or new processes improve things?

> Your review of targets should include four steps which are a continuum: set targets; plan; act; and review.

9. Aim for continuous year on year improvements

There is no going back on this one. It's what plumbers and hydraulic engineers call a non-return valve! Things can only be allowed to go one way. And every year it should get better than the last. It's not just about driving performance up: costs are supposed to be going down; service is getting better; more

Customer needs are being met; and more data are being gathered. The business is supposed to be improving in every possible way. That is one of the major benefits of driving an organisation by Customer loyalty and brings me back to one of my opening comments. Loyalty is inescapably the truth of the success of your whole business.

All Customer are not equal

A primary part of the task here is to develop mechanisms which identify and grade our Customers against their expectation and their value or potential value to the business.

Given the opportunity to communicate, share their feelings or voice an opinion, higher loyalty potential Customers often identify themselves. They respond to you and, in effect, say, "Here I am. Listen to me. Speak to me. Recognise me."

I have a Client whose marketing budget runs into tens of millions of pounds. They have a clientele some of whom could spend as much as this with them in turnover. Equally, some may not spend more than £1000 a year with them. How should this Client treat them? Are they expected to deal with small loyal spenders in exactly the same way as those businesses which spend tens of millions with them? Plainly, they are not. Even if they were crazy enough to want to, they simply could not afford to.

Matching service levels to Customers

Customers need to be graded. Some Customers will expect and understand that they will be spoken to *en masse* via television or the press. Others, will demand to be "account managed" or given personal attention. The challenge is to exceed Customer expectations at all levels profitably. Cost-to-serve is an important issue here. We are looking to increase sales from existing Customers – thus, if you are going to err, I would err on the generous side! And this is where it is helpful to have some assessment or knowledge of the actual and potential lifetime value.

I have seen businesses grade Customers by turnover, volume off-take (which I don't recommend) and by profit. Look at actual and potential. The grades need then be matched to a set of Customer service and delivery levels which exceed each

Customer's expectations, while being profitable to you. Those who spend less will expect less. If this sounds like something of a balancing act, that's fair enough because that is exactly what it is!

> Find the group of least profitable Customers and consider the minimum levels of service you want the business to deliver. Then work upwards. Make everyone aware of these service levels. If you are unsure about anything, seek feedback from Customers. For example, a motor dealer might extend free delivery and collection of vehicles being serviced to all Customers, but include a valet service only for certain others. A decision could be based on a number of individual criteria or on a blend of several, perhaps by how long they have been Customers, the number of vehicles they have purchased, or how far up the range they have bought.

Customers can go down as well as up!

Much to the dismay of some Customer-facing staff, this grading process has a hard edge. The only way is not up! Customers can be downgraded as well as upgraded: thus they may need sensitive handling when service levels decrease. Competitive service positioning should be watched to ensure that you are not withdrawing something which a competitor would be prepared to give. On the happier side, the desired direction is up, which means increasing the service levels and maintaining them. To be quite explicit about this, remember I am proposing variances in the level of service here, not the standards. The business should only have one set of service standards. It is very slippery ground indeed for one organisation to run more than one set.

> A bank marketing director spent his life jetting round Australia and had reached the highest level possible in Ansett Airlines Customer loyalty programme. Every privilege possible, he enjoyed. Then he had left Australia for his new job. A few weeks before telling the story he had returned and flew Ansett for the first time in eighteen months. "They

> didn't know who I was and I was treated as if I was a backpacker," he complained.
>
> We discussed this among the group. What the banker wanted was not unrealistic. He said, "I would have liked a letter thanking me for my business and asking if my absence from their cabins was anything to do with them. I would have liked them to say that, perhaps, they might extend my privileges for another, say, year. Or even that would let me down gently by dropping me a grade every six months. Is that unreasonable?"
>
> The take out from the session was that it's reasonable to downgrade a Customer. They understand when they are not spending with you. But how you downgrade them needs thought and understanding.

I said that downgrading can cause some upset with Customer-facing staff. It's simply that downgrading is obviously more arduous and a much less pleasant thing to do than upgrading – rather like asking a sales person to collect a late payment cheque from a Customer. Many would rather leave the debt-chasing to the accounts department! However, the company does not have a bottomless purse and it should be appreciated that those who get too much service deny others their fair share.

> Downgrade Customers sensitively and courteously. In some cases, letting them know in advance might also prove helpful. Saying "thank you" is a good idea too! This is one of those topics where asking yourself, "How would I like it done to me?", is a great idea. You can do that with price increases too. Don't just think about the message, think about the medium. A visit, phone call, letter, fax or e-mail? Which is the most appropriate?

Complaints – strange things you should know

There are some strange experiences that result from complaint handling. Firstly, and most perversely, if you successfully handle a Customer complaint and resolve the issue to their complete

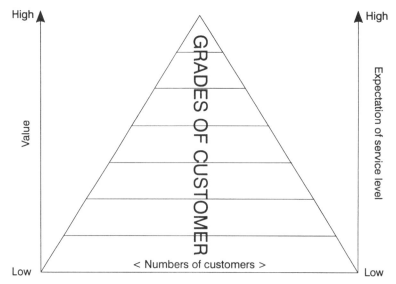

Figure 1   The pyramid of expectation. As Customer value increases so does their expectation of service. Customers can be graded by actual and/or potential sales or profit contribution.

satisfaction, that process will almost always leave you with a Customer who will demonstrate far higher levels of loyalty than a Customer who has never had a problem in the first place. Weird but true! It plainly tells you to develop a programme of upsetting Customers and then . . . don't even think about it!

> **Never fail to take any complaint seriously and to effect a resolution which leaves your Customer totally in awe of your desire to keep them, value them and respect their needs and feelings.**

When a Customer complains and no one listens they don't like it; so much so that the loyalty potential of a complainant who gets a hearing quadruples. And that's just as a result of someone listening so that they can get things of their chest. When, again, the complaint is satisfactorily resolved, the loyalty potential goes up to nine times higher than before the complaint.

THE NINE STEPS TO PROFITABLE LOYALTY BUILDING

1. There are nine steps to building and managing Customer loyalty – but they are useless without the first one. You have to create your own corporate definition of loyalty and build in measurable performance indicators.
2. You can build a profile of your most loyal Customers. Use this profile to be more discriminating about your Customer acquisition. It is perfectly possible to choose those Customers with a higher propensity to be loyal to you and leave the rest to your competitors.
3. Loyalty building will need recruitment, motivation and rewards geared to your Customer strategies and objectives. Management thinking, processes and systems have to become geared to Customer retention.
4. No Customer should defect without: you knowing about it; the Customer being able to tell you why; the business learning from it and fixing any problems.
5. Customers need to be graded. The grading must account for their potential as well as their actual value. The grading should be an active process and Customers will vary up or down as their value changes.
6. Customers' expectations rise and fall roughly in tune with their spending. Service levels should exceed their changing expectations. Service standards must not vary – but service levels should.
7. Strangely, complaints are good for business. A complaining Customer who is listened to has four times more loyalty potential. A Customer whose complaint is heard and a satisfactory resolution promptly found could become *nine times* more loyal.

How do you measure loyalty? — Chapter 4

Coming up in this chapter

> *Measuring loyalty*
> *Involving your Customers*
> *The four dimensions of loyalty*
> *Getting your team on board*

Getting the measure of loyalty

Loyalty at its heart – what people do as opposed to what people say – can be measured by their ultimate action: their buying behaviour. However to limit yourself to this is like planning a journey by the distance; you take no account of what the road is like. To get the full picture, we need to access Customers' feelings as well as their actions. The problem here is that Customers, particularly disgruntled Customers, don't talk to you; they don't share their feelings.

British Airways, who carried out their own research into this, discovered that:

- only 8% of Customers talked to their Customer relations people about the quality of service and whether their experience was good or bad
- a further 24% did share their feelings with someone but the information never reached Customer relations
- the majority, 68%, didn't talk to anybody.

As a result British Airways decided to facilitate the process and encourage Customers to talk to them in greater numbers. They set up Customer listening posts which included internationally toll free surveys, Customer forums held and attended by BA executives and actually put Customer relations personnel on flights with Customers. Their data showed then that for every £1 invested in Customer retention, they received £2 back.

Astonished by the return, British Airways re-engineered their Customer service process down from 13 steps to three; empowered their Customer relations teams to use whatever resources were required to retain their Customer; and invested in interpersonal skill training to improve the handling of Customers.

Customer complaint handling is also now a three step process at British Airways: Step 1 – apologise and get an individual to own the problem; Step 2 – resolve the complaint quickly – their target is same day, three days is the longest acceptable; Step 3 – convince the Customer that the problem is being fixed to stop it happening again. The airline endeavours to do as many as possible of the steps by phone.

Loyalty and the link to re-purchase

The following three tables are the results of a Customer survey carried out by one of my Clients. What they demonstrate is the very tangible link between loyalty and the intent to re-purchase: I see this intent as a valuable measure of loyalty.

Table 1   Customer superformance guarantees repeat sales.

Satisfaction level	Definitely/probably buy again (%)
Very satisfied	95
Satisfied	66
Less than satisfied	14

Table 2   Resolving Customers' problems is vital for future business.

Satisfaction level following problem resolution	Definitely/probably buy again (%)
Satisfied	76 (over 5 times "dissatisfied")
Mollified	34
Dissatisfied	14

Table 3   Effective problem recovery is powerfully good for sales (as well as relationships).

Satisfaction level following problem resolution	Definitely/probably buy again (%)
Satisfied (30%)	76
Mollified (50%)	34
Dissatisfied (20%)	14
Unresolved (37%)	21

HOW DO YOU MEASURE LOYALTY?

From the three tables, we can see that this Client was in a rather unhappy state and there was plenty of work to be done. Firstly, Table 1 shows that they were no different to the rest of the world. Their Customers confirmed that, if they were actively satisfied, 95% said they would buy again. Table 2 demonstrates that a satisfied Customer is more than five times likely to buy again. Table 3 shows that (bottom left) 37% of their Customer problems were unresolved at the time of the survey. This is a quite frightening figure! Taking the 100% whose problems had been resolved, 30% were satisfied, 50% were mollified and 20% were dissatisfied. I suspect the 14% of Customers expressing dissatisfaction were probably prepared to buy again because somewhere earlier, they had enjoyed a different experience and this demonstrates that Customers do have a certain degree of tolerance. Or it may just be that they don't feel that they would get any better anywhere else! The figure of the unresolved who would buy again, you will notice, is higher than those whose complaint had been resolved unsatisfactorily. That is plainly because a number of them were still waiting in line to become dissatisfied!

The figures in these tables were used widely within the organisation both to convince senior executives that they should invest heavily and quickly in their equivalent of a Customer superformance programme and to demonstrate to sales and marketing people that a rapid change of culture, style and method was vitally necessary and long overdue. The picture was probably actually worse than stated here and as revealed by the survey. My experience suggests that these figures usually overstate the case of repurchase. In the USA research confirms this: somewhere between 60 and 80% of automobile purchasers, interviewed 90 days after a purchase, said they would buy the same brand again yet, three to four years later, only 35–40% actually do. The moral is clear: stay in touch and superform at every opportunity. If the opportunities don't arise, create them.

Checklist of the most popular Customer loyalty measures

- ❏ Customer satisfaction – what they say
- ❏ Recency – when did they last purchase?

- Frequency – how often do they purchase?
- Monetary value – how much do they spend?
- Customer longevity – how long have they been with you?
- Formal and informal (word of mouth) referral activity
- Share of spend – how much to you and how much to competitors?
- Willingness to repurchase

Share of spend

Consciously work to build your share of the available and appropriate "wallet" for that family, household or business and suddenly the whole picture is transformed. If most businesses had anything like 75% of the available spend of its Customers, annual targets would be met in the first month! Most businesses neglect Customers and, as a result, Customers place business elsewhere.

When looking at how much they spend, remember to look at current and recent transactions, but keep a cumulative figure too.

When you have captured at least 75% of the Customers' available spend, you know you have secured their trust, their loyalty and their affection. "Available spend", with a business, would probably be a budget for that product or service. With a consumer, it is either their appropriate, affordable or desired amount. Often this is a notional assessment but you can easily ask the Customer.

How far will they go to help you?

Another valuable piece of information is whether that Customer will do anything positive or negative to assist you: whether they ever pass on positive or negative word of mouth; whether they are prepared to give solicited referrals or testimonials. With these questions, you are deep into the heart of "soft issue" country.

HOW DO YOU MEASURE LOYALTY?

Often you will find that Customers are more open, more honest in fact, about whether they would recommend you to someone else than they are about whether they would buy from you again.

When does loyalty get real?

The vital aspect of using Customer satisfaction as one of the measures of loyalty is that you should understand just how high the satisfaction levels need to be before Customers actually can be described as actively satisfied and start to display real loyalty. If you index Customer satisfaction from 1 to 10, don't expect a significant level of robust loyalty until you achieve beyond 8 on the scale. From 6 to 8 they are still very vulnerable to competitive offers and propositions; lower than that there is no loyalty of any value.

> People worry about how to measure Customer satisfaction – active or otherwise. They worry too about measuring share of Customer spend and about measuring future potential. How on earth can you measure these things? Easy! Ask your Customers to tell you.

And don't forget loyalty work has four dimensions!

I take the view that loyalty building, like marketing, has four dimensions. The dimensions are:

- *forward external activity directed to your market – its conventional direction*
- *reverse external activity aimed at suppliers and those with whom you have formed partnerships or alliances*
- *internal activity communicating with colleagues and staff*
- *support activity, if appropriate, to shareholders or other stakeholders.*

Thinking about suppliers

I have had very active experience of the value of building loyalty from my suppliers. And if your business is using techniques such

forty-three

as supply chain management, you may already have identified the issue with suppliers for yourself. To gear up your business to superform for its Customers without entering into the necessary close alliances and partnerships with your suppliers is futile. Within a short period of time they will seem to be living on another planet.

I often think this is like planes re-fuelling in flight. If one increased its speed and the other didn't, not a lot of fuel would get through! You and your suppliers have to be flying at the same speed!

> Talk to external suppliers and others in the chain – and, if you are one of those businesses which include internal suppliers in the chain, talk to them too. Involve everyone, and gain their commitment and support. Their loyalty will build as you work at the problems together and you share the responsibilities and benefits together. Remember the power of praise. Businesses are much better at sharing negative experiences than consumers; however businesses are much, much worse at handing out praise than they are at complaining!

Investors, too, can come into our loyalty work

The average holding time for shares by investors has tumbled from seven years in 1960 to two years in 1996. This figure underlines just how little companies do to create loyalty from their investors, which has never been more vital than it is today. Without the support and loyalty of your investors, thinking long term, or merely longer term, is a non-starter. There is absolutely nothing to stop you investing in communication programmes and loyalty building activity with your shareholders. Why shouldn't they, for example, be proud to own your shares as well as expect to make money from them? There is nothing to stop you using very similar devices as we have been discussing for Customers to analyse, measure and manage investor loyalty. A US expert suggests that retaining or regaining private ownership is the answer. This may lack a little in pragmatism, but it is right ideally. If you can't, get to work on an investor loyalty initiative – but it must build the genuine loyalty we have discussed.

HOW DO YOU MEASURE LOYALTY?

And what about your people – how loyal are they?

Loyal staff breed loyal Customers. And a company that wants to superform needs super-staff. Super employees are not created overnight. They are never super on their first day. If things go right, they improve as time passes. Customers love the experience, the product or service knowledge, and they love to deal with motivated people who admire and are loyal to their employers. Customers take comfort in that it reassures them and endorses their own good feelings or perhaps makes them see that any bad experience is an exception. And the other thing Customers love is consistency; finding the same people there, people they recognise and who recognise them.

> *I like the fact that their people know what they are talking about, they're enthusiastic and they can't do enough to help. And I've been dealing with the same team for years.*
> **– Alan Beckwith, Customer of a local garden centre**

Economically, building employee loyalty makes sense in the same way as Customer loyalty. An employer with a high turnover of staff will find recruiting new people and training them is expensive, just as recruiting new prospects and converting them to Customers is expensive. The sums of money are different, but they are both very expensive.

> **Be in no doubt, those who understand and learn and become masters of managing the four dimensions of loyalty will be amongst the most sought after and valued in the business world. Could you be one of those people?**

The development of employee loyalty is fundamental to the success of delivering a sound corporate promise. The quality of your people is vital. And the greater the reliance on technology and computerised Customer solutions, the greater, I believe, the focus is on the people, the human element of our interactions. You must, therefore, only recruit quality people and you must recognise that such people take their motivation, satisfaction and fulfilment from far more important things than just money. Another virtuous circle of Customer-driven businesses is the recognition

BUILDING CUSTOMER LOYALTY

that people who have the propensity to be loyal employees value and understand loyalty. Nothing will give them more pleasure and satisfaction than dealing with, and cultivating, that same quality in your Customers.

1. Customer loyalty is measured by:
   - ☐ Customer satisfaction
   - ☐ Recency – when did they last purchase?
   - ☐ Frequency – how often do they purchase?
   - ☐ Monetary value – how much do they spend?
   - ☐ Customer longevity – how long have they been with you?
   - ☐ Formal and informal (word of mouth) referral activity
   - ☐ Share of spend – how much to you and how much to competitors?
   - ☐ Willingness to repurchase
2. Achieving a dominant "share of Customer spend" is important. However it is of no robust significance until it hits around 75%.
3. Loyalty work is four dimensional – forward to Customers, internally to staff, externally to suppliers and even to shareholders where appropriate.
4. To be involved in a process of Customer superformance and loyalty building without the participation, involvement and support of your suppliers as well as Customers is a mistake and will yield failures.
5. You can and should work on investor loyalty. Working on long-term Customer improvements to your business is difficult without investor support and understanding. Investors will respond similarly to Customers when you market the business to them. Their loyalty can be measured in similar ways.
6. The fourth dimension of loyalty lies with your staff: quality of people is key and loyal employees value and exude loyalty and will breed loyal Customers.

The Customer-driven Business Model — Chapter 5

Coming up this chapter

Be Customer-driven
17 key issues for Customer loyalty
Formal and informal referrals

I have referred a number of times to the Customer-driven business model. And now we come to it. You can also think of it as a loyalty machine. Get your business running this way, get your act right, and Customer loyalty is the natural end result. When you look at the machine, you'll find it has four principal areas. The top area is about the acquisition of new business. The left-hand side is about looking after Customers and fulfilling all their needs. The central core — I think of it as the engine of the Customer loyalty machine — is Customer Superformance. And then to the right, are issues to do with complaint handling and resolution.

I have numbered the panels in the model (Figure 2, overleaf) and the numbers relate to the paragraphs that follow it. Effectively, now you have a step-by-step guide to building and managing real Customer loyalty: a step-by-step guide to a Customer-driven business.

The 17 key issues for Customer loyalty

This is a model for a business devoted to Customer loyalty. And you can see the additional benefits of this devotion around the sides of the model: lower costs, improved brand performance and increased business efficiency. This is a veritable treasure chest of untapped potential for your business. Look at the issues which rain (sideways rain!) on improved brand performance. On the other side, more rain! This time showering improvements to costs and meanwhile, every issue leads to eventual increased business efficiencies.

1. High focus marketing is the process of focusing on those Customers in your prospective market who have the highest potential loyalty for you. These can be modelled out from analysis of your Customer database. The strategic concept

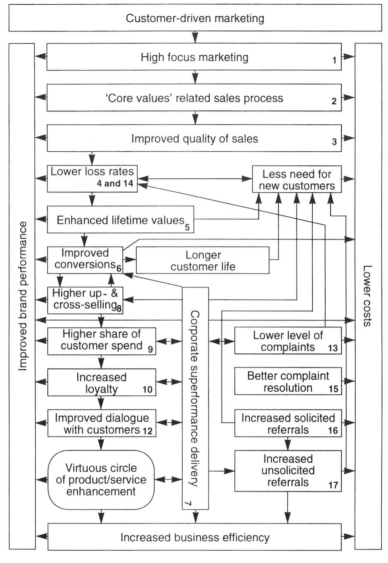

Figure 2 JFR's Customer-driven business model.

here is to secure dominant market share of those Customers who "lock" with your core corporate and brand values – the things that differentiate you from your competition; the essential you.

2. In turn, naturally, you must then embed those core values into your sales process. This optimises the "fit" between the way you attract Customers and what they want – or are buying – from you.

3. Once you get that fit, there is a dramatic improvement in the quality of the business you gain. Effectively, you are now taking the cream from the marketplace and leaving the rest for your competitors to fight over.

> **Is your plug in?**
>
> Most businesses are running the bath with the plug out. They have the taps of sales and marketing full on. They are scrabbling round in a frenzied search for new Clients. Meanwhile, because sales people are "so busy", the easiest new business to get is being missed. Customers of all grades are flooding out down the plug. Remember the European insurance company where all we did was re-focus on existing Customers and increasing loyalty? Business shot up.

4. In turn, this has two effects which will be of enormous benefit for your business: firstly, higher loyalty means lower Customer attrition; secondly, this will be a major factor in "putting the plug in". In consequence, you will cut back radically on the very high costs of hunting for new business from totally "cold" prospects.
5. Next, from the model, you can see the natural follow-on is that Customer lifetime values are enhanced. If you haven't already started calculating and using lifetime values I really must encourage you to do so. The use of lifetime values seems to be almost like turning on a light to so many of those who remain unconvinced by the ethical, moral, cultural or philosophical rationales for rebuilding their business around the Customer.
6. Once you have defined and calculated your measures of lifetime values, you can start the process of managing them and beginning to appreciate the full benefits of what can be achieved. There are two significant uplifts which you will get from managing Customer lifetime values upwards. Firstly, you will find that the conversion to sale ratios are approximately doubled. You can imagine the effect this has on sales costs. They tumble! Secondly, you will find that simply being aware of, and managing, the process of Customer lifetime values brings the in-built benefit of extending them.

Now that the light is turned on and you can really see what's what, the argument for delivering Customer superformance – actually exceeding Customer expectations with every transaction and interaction – begins to make supreme sense. It is only when you look a the financial dynamics of lifetime values that a lot of the things you must do for loyalty building become affordable. Trying to run a business devoted to Customer loyalty but costing it against single transactions doesn't work. Make the shift and the debate about whether Customers deserve, or are worth it, just falls away.

7. Now the earnest business of prolonging Customer "life" by keeping them deliriously, constantly and actively satisfied with your business, the service and values you deliver and the products which you make or distribute, should become a permanent quest which will preoccupy and obsess all staff. The obsession applies whether they are Customer facing or not. Customer superformance is a benign and wonderful concept. It must take place at every opportunity and in every area. It will bring nothing but prosperity, growth and profit to your business.
8. You are about to kick-start your business into the next phase of its development in becoming Customer driven. Those improved conversion ratios pay off with much higher incidences of cross- and up-selling to your existing Customers – the easiest, least expensive sales your business can achieve. In Chapter 6, I will explain just how dramatically this step can work for you. It is quite common for the movement of activity and resource away from "cold" conquest or prospecting to focus on existing Customers will improve return on investment by five to 15 times; an average of a ten-fold improvement.
9. With the simultaneous effect of Customer superformance and our improved conversion rates yielding more cross- and up-selling, we find the all significant share of Customer spend increases rapidly. This is a great loyalty builder and a great way of measuring the success of your loyalty work.
10. Now you will start to see the loyalty factor climbing to levels you would only ever have dreamed of before, if you had been ready or able to measure it.
11. As the natural result, you have a vastly improved dialogue with Customers and this will begin returning benefits to you. They value you because you have amply demonstrated that you care about and value them. The word "natural" here is interesting because if you look at the model you will see how naturally these steps fit together. Given that you perform and listen and deliver, everything fits holistically, harmoniously into a natural order. It is this natural quality of the process that gives it such elegance, and that makes it as right for you as it is for your Customers.

12. With the dialogue between you and your Customers enabling discussion, debate and free exchanges about their needs and feelings and encouraging honest, frank feedback regarding your efforts for them, you now arrive at a virtuous circle of product and service enhancement. With openness abounding, debate and discussion taking place, you can "sit" with your Customers and discuss the future. You can discuss what you are getting right and wrong, what they want and don't want, and what their views and feelings are. This will yield a wealth of new product and process development ideas and activities. In turn you can ask Customers for opinion and counsel. They feel involved, heard and recognised. And you can discuss all your new ideas with them.
13. Turning to the model again, observe what is happening to the right of the Customer superformance panel. Once you turn the spotlight on to amazing your Customers at every opportunity, exceeding their perception of service and value, you will find complaints plummet to all time lows. This is good news and bad news! On the one hand, it is obviously good news; Customers are happy with you and what you are doing for them. On the other hand, it is bad news because complaints, as we learned in Chapter 2, are valuable opportunities to build Customer loyalty.
14. As you manage complaint figures down, notice how this contributes to a further reduction in your Customer loss rate (on the left-hand side towards the top of the chart).
15. Handling complaints efficiently and effectively, of course, gives you valuable experience in how to react to unhappy Customers. The more you learn, the faster you act, and the better you should become at complaint resolution.
16. All of this, supported by the radically improving standards in Customer superformance, brings you another naturally flowing benefit. Moving back to the lower left panels of the chart, we see how, once we have started genuinely to work the loyalty spell, we can actually – if gently and sensitively – ask the Customer to help us. We can ask them to provide us with referrals.
17. Then, finally, we gain the full benefit of what I described earlier as the cheapest, most effective advertising you can buy: word of mouth. These are the unsolicited testimonials with which Customers reward those with whom they are wholly content, those who get it right, leaving them actively satisfied. They are so supremely happy they want to tell the world about you.

The power of word of mouth

Research published by CMT Direct about the UK motor insurance market discovered that, based on a sample of 65,000 motorists, "word of mouth" provided their business with more name awareness than television, press and direct mail put together. In fact, "word of mouth" tops the list at a tad more than 27%. Let this tell you something about what your Customers will do for you – if you get it right! They say that a happy Customer tells three or four people, and an unhappy Customer tells thirteen. This is probably why it's unlucky!

> You'll find I have used the word referral from time to time. This is the process of getting one Customer to recommend us to another, perhaps friend, family or colleague. Referrals come in two forms: formal referrals, where we have prompted or requested the Customer's assistance; and informal referrals, which is most commonly referred to as word of mouth. Both are extremely valuable, yet few people outside financial services and, for some reason, office equipment and stationery, have formal referral activity.

Notice this!

Before we finish this piece on JFR's Customer-driven business model, let me ask you to notice one or two more things. These are positively magic qualities for your business and perhaps the secret of the success of the whole concept of Customer loyalty and a Customer-driven business. At the beginning of this section I listed the additional outcomes as: improved brand performance; lower costs; and increased business efficiency. I'd like you to just look at the number of arrows which point to increased brand efficiency and equally the number which point to lower costs. And for that matter, while you're counting arrows, it wouldn't do any harm to note that there are quite a few pointing to the panel "less need for new Customers"! Also note that everything in the chart moves towards increased business efficiency. That's why I describe this process as benign, virtuous and holistic. It is as near as you

THE CUSTOMER-DRIVEN BUSINESS MODEL

will get to organic. It enhances the lives of all it touches. That is why it works. It simply returns the dynamics of the business to "reset".

> 1. Customer-driven businesses build loyalty. The Customer-driven business model describes a natural, holistic set of processes which are in harmony with Customers' needs and desires.
> 2. Following the Customer-driven business model, as well as building Customer loyalty, you will enjoy lower costs, improved brand performance, and increased business efficiency.
> 3. Word of Mouth is a valuable introducer of new business and can be managed and encouraged.

Kick-starting the Loyalty Process — Chapter 6

Coming up in this chapter

Where to start
Re-tuning your mind . . . and your money
The Time Tested Time Test

Where to start

You are almost ready to start making loyalty work for you and your business. You've learned what true loyalty is all about, you've discovered the five strands of Customer loyalty – price, product, delivery, service and recognition – and you've learned how to manage and measure loyalty, including the vital importance of retaining Customers. But where should you start and what happens when you do?

There are two places where the business will benefit enormously from your instant attention. The first is in Customer retention – putting the plug in! The more you can do to put your retention rate up and your loss rate down, the better. The second is to change the mix of sales so that a greater proportion is repeat business from existing Customers and a lower proportion is from prospecting for totally new Customers.

> One of my favourite sayings was delivered to me during a course on NLP (Neuro-Linguistic Programming). It is this:
>
> If you go on doing what you've always done,
> You'll go on getting what you've always got.
> If it's not working – CHANGE IT!
>
> How healthy is your attitude to change?

Customer loyalty by definition must come from concentrating on existing Customers and therefore we have to change the proportions of money, activity and resources in general which are

fifty-five

working for Customers. The business has to learn to become obsessed with fostering and nurturing good relationships with its Customers, rather than obsessed with foraging for new business.

Until you start looking carefully at the quality of new business coming in – whether Customers have the propensity to be loyal – it will continue to water down your efforts. So where does your new, as distinct from repeat, business come in from? The answer, of course, is your advertising, sales and marketing activity. So these have to be adjusted to target and attract Customers who match your loyal Customer profile.

Dynamic benefits from Customer loyalty

There are ultra-dynamic benefits to working on Customer loyalty. The cost of acquiring more business from existing Customers is 5–15 times less expensive than the cost of acquiring totally new business. It seems to me quite crazy if global experience tells us that you will get so much more effectiveness from time, money and effort spent on existing Customers than with "cold" activity, that we deploy most of our resources where they will achieve the least loyalty *and* the least sales. In fact, if you only moved, say, 10% of your prospecting money and effort, then by spending it wisely on existing Customers, if our experience matches even the worst of the rest of the world, we would experience the equivalent of tripling the Customer budget.

> Marketing, advertising and selling may be the three primary generators of our business intake, but think about the rest of the business too. Where else, Customer-facing or not, can the mix of resources and processes relating to their – internal or external – Customers change to achieve better effect?

But don't we need advertising to build our image and brands?
Of course, this is where the big boys who frequent the peak TV slots chip in with questions like, "But what about awareness?", or, "But what about brand building?" To which I ask why the two activities of prospect or conquest and Customer communications

can't deliver brand effects. In fact they do! But they do so in a much less wasteful, much more targeted way. Moreover, by making both prospecting and Customer communications heavily brand literate, we can pump them up to make sure they work even better than ever before.

> **The Marie Curie Story**
>
> My late father, Bernard Robinson OBE, founded the Marie Curie Memorial Foundation, more popularly recognised these days as Marie Curie Cancer Care. It's a somewhat romantic story, starting with an old lady who, when hearing his intention to start a cancer charity, took off her engagement ring and offered it to him. He sold it, as she had suggested, for about £75; in those days a reasonable sum for a first donation.
>
> My father decided to devote all of it to raising more money. So he carried out a mailing to raise funds. The amassed funds financed another mailing and so on until he had built a base of regular subscribers and enough surplus to start the serious work of fighting cancer and caring for the stricken.
>
> For years the Marie Curie continued mailing its donor list (the word database of course was not invented for years to come) twice a year and "cold" prospects mailings were despatched in millions. At one point, he had the rate well in excess of 12 million a year. There was one particularly interesting side-effect. Marie Curie achieved the top slot in brand awareness. Their unprompted figures left the others light years behind! The learning point here is that my father achieved this coveted position without spending anything on advertising. The "advertising effect" was achieved as a by-product of the mailings. It cost him nothing. And, in terms of loyalty, his Christmas appeal to his hundreds of thousands of existing donors would pull a 40–45% response. Cold mailings in contrast would pull around 3%. This is a graphic demonstration both of the value and effect of loyalty.

The Marie Curie story clearly demonstrates what many advertising traditionalists have been reluctant to admit. Direct mail, like many of the other marketing disciplines, can have a powerful effect on brand building and brand equity and make an equally strong contribution to the effects of advertising and loyalty building. In fact, the brand is delivered throughout your business. No amount of advertising will do you any good if the product is rubbish or your people are rude. The big point is that you only want brand delivery to people who you might want as Customers. Leaving aside corporate image, why do you want to spread your brand gospel to people who you do not want to buy or who have no influence on buyers?

However, it would be utterly foolish to believe that our brand, corporate or product efforts need neither advertising nor marketing because our Customer and prospecting activities are so brand conscious and so brand powerful. Yet there is a strong case that budgets should be drastically reduced in this area. The power of what we might still describe as the "mass media" – by which I mean they cover slabs of our market *en masse* – can affect both existing and prospective Customers. The question really is how much more you can achieve when you strap brand work to other targeted Customer or prospecting activity or communications rather than leave it to advertising. And the answer is you can achieve miracles!

What we forgot to remember

Focus your thoughts solely on existing Customers and conquest or prospecting for the next few moments. In *High Performance Sales Management* I listed the best way to prioritise sales activity. I will call it the Time Tested Time Test. It is quite simply "knowledge" that has been handed down almost since selling began. In this form it is applicable to financial consumer markets but actually, if anything, it applies equally or perhaps even more to most other consumer, professional and business markets and anyone can adapt it to their own situation. It is basically a list, in descending order, of the most effective places you can spend your time if you want to end up with a big fat order book. To sales people this is one of those crazy things which they all know is right, but they have enormous trouble switching off that damn machine which seems to have been built in to them; the one that instructs them to seek out totally new Customers; the one that teaches them that a wealth of new Customers is some kind of Holy Grail which they should head for.

There are big, big savings here

The claim that you can increase sales and marketing productivity is not a wild or crazy claim. It is quite simply the reward you will get from re-focusing the business on what will do the most good for it. This is, with no word of exaggeration, probably the single largest miracle that you can perform for your business. What you have read in this book has, quite literally, enabled me to turn companies round. In one notable case, we achieved massive increases in sales which almost defied explanation, while simultaneously cutting sales and marketing spending by huge amounts. And Customers loved it; they must have, or it wouldn't have worked. And all this comes about through loyalty work.

> Ask yourself these three questions:
>
> ❏ Why do we spend so little of the total of our sales and marketing cash and resource on existing Customer when time honoured wisdom and many decades of experience by direct and other marketers guarantee us significantly higher returns in terms of sales, Customer retention and loyalty?
> ❏ Why do we spend so much of our sales and marketing money and effort on finding new business when everyone accepts that prospecting and conquest business is the hardest and most expensive thing we can do and is usually totally devoid of any selectivity about who we most want for our Customers?
> ❏ Why do we not achieve significant brand-building through all our Customer and prospecting activity and communications when these can achieve so much for so little cost and to such great effect?

My experience and belief is that most businesses can save 25–40% of their sales, marketing and advertising costs and activity simply by re-focusing their effort to the place where it can do the most good for the lowest cost; all by concentrating on building Customer loyalty. Those savings could go straight to the bottom line. Or you might have some better things to do with it!

Nothing could, of course, be further from the truth. Direct marketers have proved it time and time again for 40 or more years. They experience massive differences in response and cost effectiveness between their own Customer lists and the "cold" lists they rent in. And cold lists is what direct marketers appropriately call them. Sales people, too, have experienced this across time and there are even jokes about the infamous drudge of cold calling. So look at the list below from a higher level. See how, the further away we get from existing Customers, the less fertile the ground gets, the harder it is to make sales or contribute to Customer loyalty. Here's the list:

The Time Tested Time Test
1. *Visit and review existing Customers*
2. *Other visits to existing Customers (courtesy and service calls)*
3. *Family referrals (in business to business, colleague referrals and to other businesses)*
4. *Other referrals*
5. *Orphans (Customers currently unassigned to sales people or intermediaries)*
6. *Lapsed Customers*
7. *Other corporate leads and promotions*
8. *"Cold" activities*

This list is used by sales managers to help their sales people evaluate the focus or investment of their time and effort. It works perfectly for prioritising loyalty building activity too. Notice particularly that it is only when you reach items 7 and 8 that you begin to step beyond the influence of Customers.

> Here is your rationale for re-focusing resource into those areas. Moving resource from Customer acquisition to Customer development and growth – concentrating on loyalty building by improving Customer relationships – increases your share of Customer spend, thus increasing sales and decreasing Customer attrition simultaneously. Now, and it can be quite suddenly, we find our costs decreasing and our business targets are more easily achieved. Indeed, we can find ourselves in the luxurious position of deciding just how much prospecting we need. You will find that you need far less than before. You even become choosy about the quality of Customer you want.

KICK-STARTING THE LOYALTY PROCESS

> Pinch yourself! Still there? You have just read how, by building Customer retention, getting the new business mix right and concentrating on loyalty, you can cut advertising, sales and marketing expenditure by huge amounts – typically 25–40% – and send sales soaring through the roof into the bargain! Got the message?

Why be a Customer-driven business?

Making loyalty work is about becoming a Customer-driven business. I would love to urge you to become a Customer-driven business because it is ethically, morally and sensibly the right thing to be. But I am aware that some of the people who run businesses will need a financial reason to do it. Do companies that care about their Customers make more money? Do companies that devote their whole being to Customer loyalty make more money? Do Customer-driven businesses make more money? My view, in answering all three questions, is that they do. And, if you follow the advice in this book, substantially more.

The mistake, if I may point it out, is to sit around trying to calculate exactly how much more. That takes time. You have to get all the building blocks in place and then calculate the difference each one makes. While you do that the zealots and the evangelists among your competitors will overtake you at the speed of light. If you have any lingering doubts about the power of Customer loyalty, just go round the Customer-driven business model again. Nobody has been able to challenge it yet.

No kidding – you're about to make a fortune!

This is potentially by far the most profitable book you have ever read. I promise you, making loyalty work can return you at least thousands of times what you have paid for this book – and, if you are spending millions, then it could quite easily return its cover price a million times over. You may find it hard to believe that this little book can hold such a big promise. But it does.

You don't have to be incredibly clever or skilled to achieve the kind of results I'm talking about, but, on behalf of the business, it does take courage. It takes courage not because I have proposed that you take any risks: simply, because people – marketing people or other senior management – *believe* it will involve risk. This is only because they have always been doing what they have been doing, have been accepting that the activities of the past were right or necessary, when really they were neither. But mostly because times have changed.

Get going!

I started this book by saying that Customer loyalty was the hottest topic of the day. And so it is! Why? Because it is the most powerful, dynamic and profitable way to turbo-charge a business and because it forces every aspect of the business to meet new challenges and win. There is no other step you can take, no other avenue which, if you can pull it off, will so dramatically improve the fortunes of a business.

> *All the answers are in JFR's Customer-driven business model. It's all very basic. All common sense. But it will challenge every system, every process, every belief and every person in my company to greater heights than we have ever been challenged before. It's incredibly exciting. Incredibly stimulating. Great!*
> **– Ralph Morgan, CEO, Morgan Financial Group.**

And so we draw to the end of this chapter and the end of this book. I trust you have enjoyed the read and that I have given you all you need to become masterly at developing and managing Customer loyalty. As you may have picked up earlier, the book is one of a series in which we are covering a combination of the hot topics and old favourites. Look out for *Effective Direct Mail* and *High Performance Sales Management*, *Mastering Motivation* and future books on marketing a small business, running meetings, key account management and copywriting. Remember, we welcome stories and experiences via e-mail at jfr@jfr.co.uk. Our website is at www.x-s.co.uk/members/jfr.

We'll close as usual with the chapter summary – holding one last thought back until the very end.

KICK-STARTING THE LOYALTY PROCESS

1. Measure and manage Customer loyalty.
2. The two most important places to get to work: put the plug in – get Customer retention sorted; and get the mix right – get a much greater proportion of business through up- and cross-selling
3. Become obsessed with nurturing Customer relationships.
4. Loyalty work brings an ultra-dynamic benefit. Sales to existing Customers are typically 5–15 times cheaper and easier than prospecting.
5. Re-target your prospecting to attract and win Customers that match your most loyal Customers' profile – they will have a greater propensity to be loyal to you.
6. Ensure that both your prospecting and Customer communications are as brand literate as possible and ask yourself whether you need to use anything like as much comparatively untargeted advertising, marketing or sales activity
7. Use the Time Tested Time Test to re-prioritise loyalty work and all sales and marketing investment and resources.
8. Don't waste time trying to calculate the financial benefits of becoming Customer-driven and dedicating yourself to loyalty – your competitors will overtake you at the speed of light.

And absolutely the last thought:

> The Customer is a Holy Cow.
> You don't milk a Holy Cow,
> You worship it.